Editor
Cristina Krysinski, M. Ed.

Editor in Chief
Karen J. Goldfluss, M.S. Ed.

Creative Director
Sarah M. Fournier

Cover Artist
Barbara Lorseyedi

Art Coordinator
Renée Mc Elwee

Imaging
Amanda R. Harter

Publisher
Mary D. Smith, M.S. Ed.

TCR 8236

Comprehe...
Using Literal, Inferential & Applied Questioning

Twenty texts presented in a variety of genres with activities to reinforce close reading

Related comprehension strategies activities for each unit

Three levels of questioning to improve comprehension and critical-thinking skills

★ Correlated to the Common Core State Standards

Teacher Created Resources

For correlations to the Common Core State Standards, see page 109 of this book or visit *http://www.teachercreated.com/standards*.

Teacher Created Resources
6421 Industry Way
Westminster, CA 92683
www.teachercreated.com

ISBN: 978-1-4206-8236-6

© 2015 Teacher Created Resources
Made in U.S.A.

Teacher Created Resources

Table of Contents

Introduction

Twenty different texts from a variety of genres are included in this reading comprehension resource. These may include humor, fantasy, myth/legend, folktale, mystery, adventure, suspense, fairy tale, play, fable, science fiction, poetry, and informational/nonfiction texts, such as a timetable, letter, report, procedure, poster, map, program, book cover, and cartoon.

Three levels of questions are used to indicate the reader's comprehension of each text.

One or more particular comprehension strategies have been chosen for practice with each text.

Each unit is five pages long and consists of the following resources and strategies:

- teacher information: includes the answer key and extension suggestions
- text page: text is presented on one full page
- activity page 1: covers literal and inferential questions
- activity page 2: covers applied questions
- applying strategies: focuses on a chosen comprehension strategy/strategies

Teacher Information

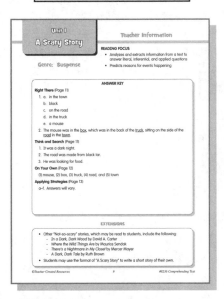

Text Page

- **Reading Focus** states the comprehension skill emphasis for the unit.

- **Genre** is clearly indicated.

- **Answer Key** is provided. For certain questions, answers will vary, but suggested answers are given.

- **Extension Activities** suggest other authors or book titles. Other literacy activities relating to the text are suggested.

- The title of the text is provided.

- Statement is included in regard to the genre.

- Text is presented on a full page.

Activity Page 1

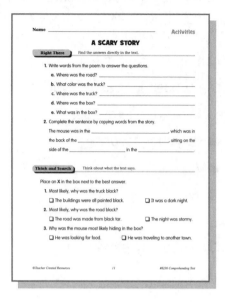

Activity Page 2

- **Right There** consists of literal questions.
- **Think and Search** consists of inferential questions.

- **On Your Own** consists of applied questions.

Applying Strategies

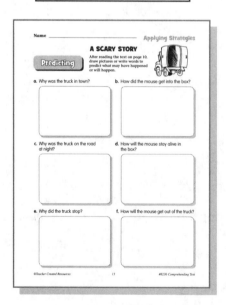

- Comprehension strategy focus is clearly labeled.
- Activities provide opportunities to utilize the particular strategy.

Types of Questions

Students are given **three types of questions** (all grouped accordingly) to assess their comprehension of a particular text in each genre:

- **Literal questions (Right There)** are questions for which answers can be found directly in the text.

- **Inferential questions (Think and Search)** are questions for which answers are implied in the text and require the reader to think a bit more deeply about what he or she has just read.

- **Applied questions (On Your Own)** are questions that require the reader to think even further about the text and incorporate personal experiences and knowledge to answer them.

Answers for literal questions are always given and may be found on the Teacher Information pages. Answers for inferential questions are given when appropriate. Applied questions are best checked by the teacher following, or in conjunction with, a class discussion.

Comprehension Strategies

Several specific comprehension strategies have been selected for practice in this book.

Although specific examples have been selected, often other strategies, such as scanning, are used in conjunction with those indicated, even though they may not be stated. Rarely does a reader use only a single strategy to comprehend a text.

Strategy Definitions

Predicting	Prediction involves the students using illustrations, text, or background knowledge to help them construct meaning. Students might predict what texts could be about, what could happen, or how characters could act or react. Prediction may occur before, during, and after reading, and it can be adjusted during reading.
Making Connections	Students comprehend texts by linking their prior knowledge with the new information from the text. Students may make connections between the text and themselves, between the new text and other texts previously read, and between the text and real-world experiences.
Comparing	This strategy is closely linked to the strategy of making connections. Students make comparisons by thinking more specifically about the similarities and differences between the connections being made.
Sensory Imaging	Sensory imaging involves students utilizing all five senses to create mental images of passages in the text. Students also use their personal experiences to create these images. The images may help students make predictions, form conclusions, interpret information, and remember details.

Strategy Definitions *(cont.)*

Determining Importance/ Identifying Main Idea(s)

The strategy of determining importance is particularly helpful when students try to comprehend informational texts. It involves students determining the important theme or main idea of particular paragraphs or passages.

As students become effective readers, they will constantly ask themselves what is most important in a phrase, sentence, paragraph, chapter, or whole text. To determine importance, students will need to use a variety of information, such as the purpose for reading, their knowledge of the topic, background experiences and beliefs, and understanding of the text format.

Skimming

Skimming is the strategy of looking quickly through texts to gain a general impression or overview of the content. Readers often use this strategy to quickly assess whether a text, or part of it, will meet their purpose. Because this book deals predominantly with comprehension after reading, skimming has not been included as one of the major strategies.

Scanning

Scanning is the strategy of quickly locating specific details, such as dates, places, or names, or those parts of the text that support a particular point of view. Scanning is often used, but not specifically mentioned, when used in conjunction with other strategies.

Synthesizing/Sequencing

Synthesizing is the strategy that enables students to collate a range of information in relation to the text. Students recall information, order details, and piece information together to make sense of the text. Synthesizing/sequencing helps students to monitor their understanding. Synthesizing involves connecting, comparing, determining importance, posing questions, and creating images.

Summarizing/Paraphrasing

Summarizing involves the processes of recording key ideas, main points, or the most important information from a text. Summarizing or paraphrasing reduces a larger piece of text to the most important details.

Genre Definitions

Fiction and Poetry

Science Fiction These stories include backgrounds or plots based upon possible technology or inventions, experimental medicine, life in the future, environments drastically changed, alien races, space travel, genetic engineering, dimensional portals, or changed scientific principles. Science fiction encourages readers to suspend some of their disbelief and examine alternate possibilities.

Suspense Stories of suspense aim to make the reader feel fear, disgust, or uncertainty. Many suspense stories have become classics. These include *Frankenstein* by Mary Shelley, *Dracula* by Bram Stoker, and *Dr. Jekyll and Mr. Hyde* by Robert Louis Stevenson.

Mystery Stories from this genre focus on the solving of a mystery. Plots of mysteries often revolve around a crime. The hero must solve the mystery, overcoming unknown forces or enemies. Stories about detectives, police, private investigators, amateur sleuths, spies, thrillers, and courtroom dramas usually fall into this genre.

Fable A fable is a short story that states a moral. Fables often use talking animals or animated objects as the main characters. The interaction of the animals or animated objects reveals general truths about human nature.

Fairy Tale These tales are usually about elves, dragons, goblins, fairies, or magical beings and are often set in the distant past. Fairy tales usually begin with the phrase "Once upon a time . . ." and end with the words ". . . and they lived happily ever after." Charms, disguises, and talking animals may also appear in fairy tales.

Fantasy A fantasy may be any text or story removed from reality. Stories may be set in nonexistent worlds, such as an elf kingdom, on another planet, or in alternate versions of the known world. The characters may not be human (dragons, trolls, etc.) or may be humans who interact with non-human characters.

Folktale Stories that have been passed from one generation to the next by word of mouth rather than by written form are folktales. Folktales may include sayings, superstitions, social rituals, legends, or lore about the weather, animals, or plants.

Play Plays are specific pieces of drama, usually enacted on a stage by actors dressed in makeup and appropriate costumes.

Genre Definitions *(cont.)*

Fiction and Poetry *(cont.)*

Adventure
Exciting events and actions feature in these stories. Character development, themes, or symbolism are not as important as the actions or events in an adventure story.

Humor
Humor involves characters or events that promote laughter, pleasure, or humor in the reader.

Poetry
This genre utilizes rhythmic patterns of language. The patterns include meter (high- and low-stressed syllables), syllabication (the number of syllables in each line), rhyme, alliteration, or a combination of these. Poems often use figurative language.

Myth
A myth explains a belief, practice, or natural phenomenon and usually involves gods, demons, or supernatural beings. A myth does not necessarily have a basis in fact or a natural explanation.

Legend
Legends are told as though the events were actual historical events. Legends may or may not be based on an elaborated version of a historical event. Legends are usually about human beings, although gods may intervene in some way throughout the story.

Nonfiction

Report
Reports are written documents describing the findings of an individual or group. They may take the form of a newspaper report, sports report, or police report, or a report about an animal, person, or object.

Letter
These are written conversations sent from one person to another. Letters usually begin with a greeting, contain the information to be related, and conclude with a farewell signed by the sender.

Procedure
Procedures tell how to make or do something. They use clear, concise language and command verbs. A list of materials required to complete the procedure is included, and the instructions are set out in easy-to-follow steps.

Other **informational texts**, such as **timetables**, **posters**, **programs**, and **maps**, are excellent sources to teach and assess comprehension skills. Highly visual texts, such as **book covers** and **cartoons**, have been included to provide the reader with other comprehension cues and are less reliant on word recognition.

Genre: Suspense

READING FOCUS

- Analyzes and extracts information from a text to answer literal, inferential, and applied questions
- Predicts reasons for events happening

ANSWER KEY

Right There (Page 11)

1. a. in the town
   b. black
   c. on the road
   d. in the truck
   e. a mouse

2. The mouse was in the <u>box</u>, which was in the back of the <u>truck</u>, sitting on the side of the <u>road</u> in the <u>town</u>.

Think and Search (Page 11)

1. It was a dark night.

2. The road was made from black tar.

3. He was looking for food.

On Your Own (Page 12)

(1) mouse, (2) box, (3) truck, (4) road, and (5) town

Applying Strategies (Page 13)

a–f. Answers will vary.

EXTENSIONS

- Other "Not-so-scary" stories, which may be read to students, include the following:
  - *In a Dark, Dark Wood* by David A. Carter
  - *Where the Wild Things Are* by Maurice Sendak
  - *There's a Nightmare in My Closet* by Mercer Mayer
  - *A Dark, Dark Tale* by Ruth Brown
- Students may use the format of "A Scary Story" to write a short story of their own.

Name _____

Read the suspense story and answer the questions on the following pages.

In a black, black town

Was a black, black road.

On the black, black road

Was a black, black truck.

In the black, black truck

Was a black, black box.

In the black, black box

Was a . . . mouse!

A SCARY STORY

Right There   Find the answers directly in the text.

1. Write words from the poem to answer the questions.

   a. Where was the road? _____

   b. What color was the truck? _____

   c. Where was the truck? _____

   d. Where was the box? _____

   e. What was in the box? _____

2. Complete the sentence by copying words from the story.

   The mouse was in the _____, which was in

   the back of the _____, sitting on the

   side of the _____ in the _____.

Think and Search   Think about what the text says.

Place an **X** in the box next to the best answer.

1. Most likely, why was the truck black?

   ☐ The buildings were all painted black.   ☐ It was a dark night.

2. Most likely, why was the road black?

   ☐ The road was made from black tar.   ☐ The night was stormy.

3. Why was the mouse most likely hiding in the box?

   ☐ He was looking for food.   ☐ He was traveling to another town.

A SCARY STORY

On Your Own   Use what you know about the text and your own experience.

Number the pictures from **1** to **5** (**1** being the smallest thing and **5** the biggest thing).

SMALLEST TO BIGGEST

A SCARY STORY

After reading the text on page 10, draw pictures or write words to predict what may have happened or will happen.

a. Why was the truck in town?

b. How did the mouse get into the box?

c. Why was the truck on the road at night?

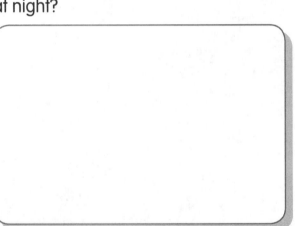

d. How will the mouse stay alive in the box?

e. Why did the truck stop?

f. How will the mouse get out of the truck?

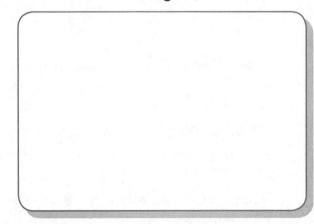

Genre: Mystery

READING FOCUS

- Analyzes and extracts information from a mystery text to answer literal, inferential, and applied questions
- Predicts future actions based on prior knowledge and reading of the text

ANSWER KEY

Right There (Page 16)

1. a. No
   b. Yes
   c. Yes
2. 4 animals

Think and Search (Page 16)

1. Drawings will vary. Possible answer(s): Picture of Crocodile.
2. Answers will vary. Possible answer(s): Crocodile left the boat on the riverbank to catch his dinner.

On Your Own (Page 17)

1. **Heaviest**   Elephant - Lion - Tiger - Monkey   **Lightest**
2. Answers will vary.

Applying Strategies (Page 18)

1. a. Drawing of an empty boat
   b. Drawing of Lion in the boat
   c. Drawing of Lion and Monkey in the boat
   d. Drawing of Lion, Monkey, and Tiger in the boat
   e. Drawing of Lion, Monkey, Tiger, and Elephant in the boat
   f. Drawings will vary.
2. Answers will vary.

EXTENSIONS

- Students can add their own actions and perform the story as a play.
- Students can create a mural of the animals in the story and other jungle animals.
- Use the story as the basis for text innovation. Students can write a similar story using the same format. For example, "Who left the clothes on the bathroom floor?"

Name _____

Read the mystery and answer the questions on the following pages.

Who left the boat on the riverbank?

Lion, did you leave the boat on the riverbank?

No, I did not leave the boat on the riverbank, but I'll get in.

Monkey, did you leave the boat on the riverbank?

No, I did not leave the boat on the riverbank, but I'll hop in.

Tiger, did you leave the boat on the riverbank?

No, I did not leave the boat on the riverbank, but I'll jump in.

Elephant, did you leave the boat on the riverbank?

No, I did not leave the boat on the riverbank, but I'll climb in.

Crocodile, did you leave the boat on the riverbank?

Yes, I left the boat on the riverbank . . . to catch my dinner!

ON THE RIVERBANK

Right There   Find the answers directly in the text.

1. Read each sentence. Choose **Yes** or **No**.

    a. Crocodile got into the boat.   ☐ Yes ☐ No

    b. Tiger got into the boat.   ☐ Yes ☐ No

    c. Crocodile left the boat on the riverbank. ☐ Yes ☐ No

2. How many animals got in the boat? _____

Think and Search   Think about what the text says.

1. Draw who you think was the cleverest animal in the story.

[ ]

2. What did he or she do?

_____

_____

_____

_____

ON THE RIVERBANK

On Your Own   Use what you know about the text and your own experience.

1. Draw the animals in the boat in order from heaviest to lightest.

Heaviest ———————————————→ Lightest

2. Do you think the boat will sink?   ❑ Yes   ❑ No

Explain why or why not.

_____

_____

_____

ON THE RIVERBANK

After reading the text on page 15, draw pictures or write words to predict what may have happened or will happen.

1. Read each sentence, and complete the picture to match each caption.

a. The boat is on the riverbank.

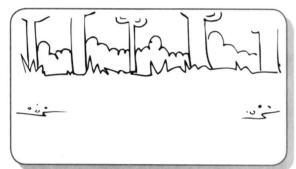

b. Lion gets in.

c. Monkey hops in.

d. Tiger jumps in.

e. Elephant climbs in.

f. Draw what happens next.

2. Write a sentence to match your prediction.

_____

_____

Genre: Informational Text—Program

READING FOCUS

- Analyzes and extracts information from a program to answer literal, inferential, and applied questions
- Makes connections between new text and his/her own experiences
- Scans text to locate words

ANSWER KEY

Right There (Page 21)

1. a. No   b. Yes   c. Yes   d. No   e. Yes

2. Friday

Think and Search (Page 21)

1. a. True   b. False   c. True

2. Mr. Wilson

On Your Own (Page 22)

1. a.   Drawings will vary.

    b–d. Answers will vary.

2. a–b. Answers will vary.

Applying Strategies (Page 23)

1. Drawing should include students performing the play.

2. a. Answers will vary.

    b. Answers will vary.

    c. Drawing should include picture of student and classmates performing the play mentioned in the previous question (2a).

EXTENSIONS

- Brainstorm information to create a program for a recent school assembly, and include details about the order of events and who did what. Compare this assembly with the one at Sunnywell Elementary School by listing similarities and differences.

- Read different fairy tales and discuss the parts played by various characters, how they would speak and move, the costumes they might wear, and the role of the storyteller.

Name _____

Read the program and answer the questions on the following pages.

Sunnywell Elementary School

Assembly Program
Friday, August 5

Presented By:	First Grade Class
Welcome:	Luke
National Anthem:	Mr. Wilson (piano)
Announcements:	Mrs. Andrews (teacher)
School Song:	Rachel
Awards:	Mr. Green (principal)
Presentation:	The Three Billy Goats Gruff First Grade Students
Thank You:	Ben

SCHOOL ASSEMBLY

Right There   Find the answers directly in the text.

1. Read each sentence. Choose **Yes** or **No**.

   a. Mrs. Andrews is the principal.   ❑ Yes   ❑ No

   b. The first grade class is presenting the assembly. ❑ Yes   ❑ No

   c. Ben is going to say thank you at the end.   ❑ Yes   ❑ No

   d. Mr. Green will make the announcements.   ❑ Yes   ❑ No

   e. Mr. Wilson plays the piano.   ❑ Yes   ❑ No

2. What day of the week will the assembly be held?

   _____

Think and Search   Think about what the text says.

1. Read each sentence. Decide if each statement is **True** or **False**.

   a. Luke and Ben are first grade students.   ❑ True   ❑ False

   b. The school song was performed by a teacher. ❑ True   ❑ False

   c. The first grade class performed a play.   ❑ True   ❑ False

2. Looking at the illustration on page 20, who do you think is in that picture?

   _____

SCHOOL ASSEMBLY

On Your Own   Use what you know about the text and your own experience.

1. **a.** Draw a picture of your principal.

b. My principal's name is _____.

c. Where is your principal in your drawing?

_____

d. What did you draw your principal doing?

_____

_____

2. Complete these sentences about your principal.

a. My principal is _____.

b. I think my principal _____.

SCHOOL ASSEMBLY

 **Making Connections**

After reading the text on page 20, draw pictures and write words to make the connection between what you already know and the new information from the text.

1. The first grade class presentation was the play about the "Three Billy Goats Gruff." Draw a picture of the children performing this play.

```



```

2. **a.** What play would you like to do? _____

b. What part would you like to play? _____

c. Draw you and some classmates performing this play.

```



```

Genre: Informational Text—Poster

READING FOCUS

- Analyzes and extracts information from a poster to answer literal, inferential, and applied questions
- Makes connections between text and personal experience
- Makes predictions by determining the importance of information in a text

ANSWER KEY

Right There (Page 26)

1. a. Hilltop Elementary School
   b. school courtyard
   c. Friday, April 15
   d. 1:00 p.m.
2. a. 5   b. 1   c. 2   d. 6

Think and Search (Page 26)

1. a. rabbit
   b. cat
   c. dog
2. Drawings will vary.

On Your Own (Page 27)

1–5. Answers will vary.

Applying Strategies (Page 28)

1. Answers/drawings will vary.
2. Drawing should show a pet on the loose.

EXTENSIONS

- Students can work in groups to create posters to advertise real or imagined events at school, such as the school sports day, events for spirit week, a class fieldtrip, or a school assembly.
- Students can view posters around the school and local community and discuss what the information on them means.

Name _____

Read the poster and answer the questions on the following pages.

Pet Parade

Hilltop Elementary School

When: Friday, April 15
Where: School courtyard
Time: 1:00 p.m.

So ... get your pet ready for the pet parade!
Show us something special your pet can do.

Win! Win! Win! PRIZES GALORE!

❖ Best groomed pet   ❖ Best tricks

❖ Best behaved pet   ❖ Best dressed pet

❖ Funniest pet   ❖ Happiest pet

Pets must be brought on a leash or in a container of some kind.

PET PARADE

Right There   Find the answers directly in the text.

1. Find the answers on the poster.

   a. Who is having a pet parade? _____

   b. Where will the pet parade be? _____

   c. What date will it be on? _____

   d. What time will it start? _____

2. Circle the correct number.

   a. How many pets are on the poster?   1   2   5   6

   b. How many dogs are on the poster?   1   2   5   6

   c. How many fish are on the poster?   1   2   5   6

   d. How many prizes are there?   1   2   5   6

Think and Search   Think about what the text says.

1. Place an **X** in the box next to the best answer.

   a. Which pet can hop?   ❏ dog   ❏ rabbit   ❏ cat

   b. Which pet can purr?   ❏ fish   ❏ rabbit   ❏ cat

   c. Which pet would like to chew on a bone? ❏ cat   ❏ dog   ❏ fish

2. Draw another pet for the poster.

PET PARADE

Give each pet a name.

1. fish 1 _____

2. fish 2 _____

3. cat _____

4. rabbit _____

5. dog _____

Name _____

PET PARADE

Making Connections

After reading the text on page 25, complete the following by making the connection between what you already know and the new information from the text.

1. Fill out the form to enter your pet in the pet parade. It can be a pet you own or one from your imagination.

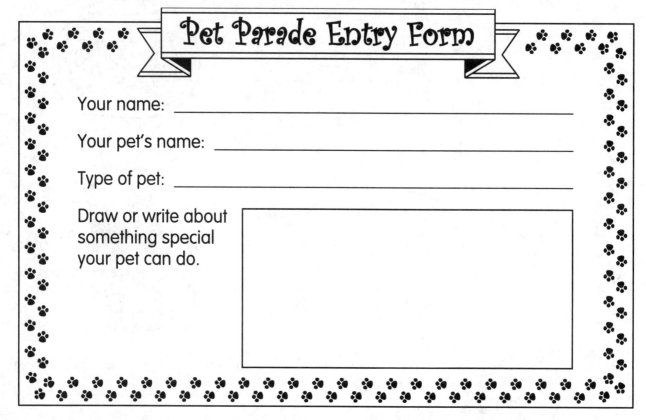

Pet Parade Entry Form

Your name: _____

Your pet's name: _____

Type of pet: _____

Draw or write about something special your pet can do.

2. Draw and write about what could happen if people forgot to put their pet on a leash or in a container.

_____

_____

_____

_____

_____

_____

28

Teacher Information

Genre: Informational
Text—Map

READING FOCUS

- Analyzes and extracts information from a map to answer literal, inferential, and applied questions
- Makes connections between a visual text and personal experience

ANSWER KEY

Right There (Page 31)

1. a. windows or teacher's desk
   b. sink or hooks
   c. heater
   d. rug/board/cupboard/windows

2. a. 1   b. 20   c. 2

3. a. Yes   b. No   c. Yes

Think and Search (Page 31)

1. Answers will vary.
2. In the sink

On Your Own (Page 32)

1. Drawings will vary.
2. Drawings and answers will vary.

Applying Strategies (Page 33)

Drawings will vary.

EXTENSIONS

- Students can work in pairs and use the maps they created to ask questions of each other, such as the relative positions of objects on their maps.
- Students can view maps created by the teacher or make their own of the school, school playground, a bedroom, or a park.

CLASSROOM

Name _____

Look at the map and answer the questions on the following pages.

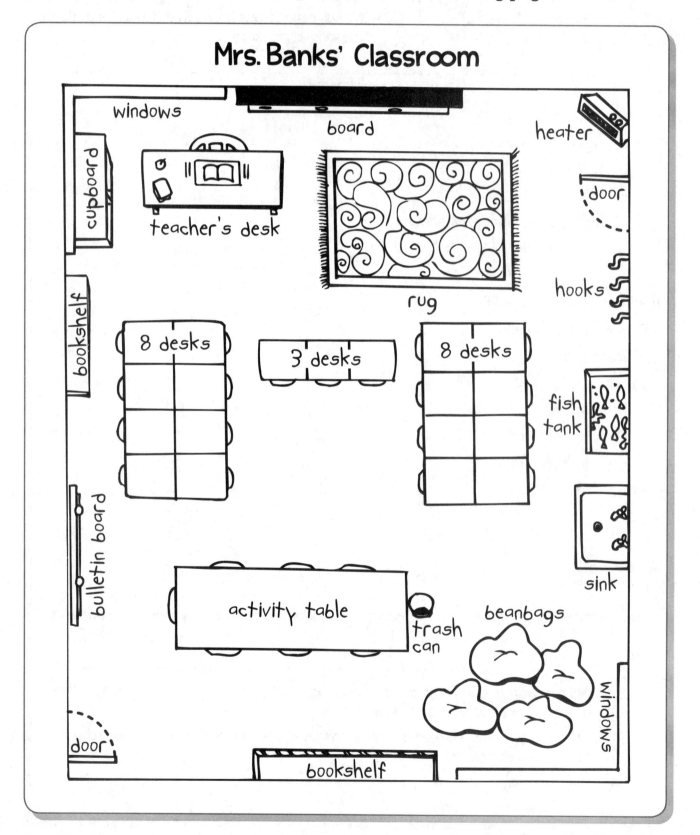

Mrs. Banks' Classroom

windows

board

heater

cupboard

teacher's desk

door

rug

hooks

bookshelf

8 desks

3 desks

8 desks

fish tank

bulletin board

activity table

trash can

beanbags

sink

windows

door

bookshelf

CLASSROOM

| **Right There** | Find the answers directly in the text. |

1. Choose a label from the map.

   a. A cupboard is in front of the _____.

   b. The fish tank is next to the _____.

   c. The _____ is behind a door.

   d. The teacher's desk is near the _____.

2. Answer the following questions.

   a. How many trash cans are in the classroom? _____

   b. How many desks are in the classroom? _____

   c. How many doors are in the classroom? _____

3. Read each question. Choose **Yes** or **No**.

   a. Is the bulletin board near the activity table?   ❑ Yes ❑ No

   b. Is the rug in front of the bookshelf?   ❑ Yes ❑ No

   c. Are the windows in the corners?   ❑ Yes ❑ No

| **Think and Search** | Think about what the text says. |

1. Where would be a good place to read a book?

_____

2. Where could you wash your hands?

_____

CLASSROOM

On Your Own   Use what you know about the text and your own experience.

1. Draw two things that you will not find in a classroom.

2. Draw and write a sentence for what may happen at the activity table.

_____

_____

CLASSROOM

Making Connections

Make a map of a classroom using the pictures below.
Draw any other items you would like on your map.

sink

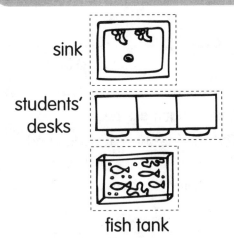

students' desks

fish tank

teacher's desk

beanbags

rug

READING FOCUS

- Analyzes and extracts information from a fairy tale to answer literal, inferential, and applied questions
- Makes connections between new text and other known texts and his/her own experiences
- Creates and recreates sensory images

ANSWER KEY

Right There (Page 36)

1. a. smile   b. looked   c. fell

2. a. Snow White—seven dwarfs

    b. Goldilocks—three bears

    c. Little Red Riding Hood—the woods

Think and Search (Page 36)

1. Yes   2. Yes   3. No   4. No   5. Answers will vary.

On Your Own (Page 37)

1. Drawings will vary.   2. Answers will vary.   3. Answers will vary.

Applying Strategies (Page 38)

1. a. Answers will vary. Possible answer(s): seven dwarfs, Snow White, three little pigs, Little Red Riding Hood, Goldilocks, three bears, woods, house, lake.

    b. Answers will vary. Possible answer(s): sad, happy.

    c. Answers will vary. Possible answer(s):

      touch—grass, trees, the water in the lake.

      smell—grass, flowers.

      hear—his friends talking, his friends laughing, birds chirping, the splash of the water.

2. Drawings and answers will vary.

EXTENSIONS

- Brainstorm ideas and create a poster or collage about "things that make people smile."
- Read different fairy tales and discuss various features. For example, how they start and finish, the good and bad characters, and the things they do.
- Play "Who am I?" giving the students clues about well-known fairy-tale characters to identify.

Name _____

Read the fairy tale and answer the questions on the following pages.

The Sad Goblin

Once upon a time, there was a very sad goblin named Sam who lost his smile. He looked and looked, but he could not find it.

He came upon seven dwarfs and Snow White and asked, "Have you seen my smile?"

"No, but we'll help you look for it," they said.

He came upon three little pigs building houses and asked, "Have you seen my smile?"

"No, but we'll help you look for it," they said.

He came upon Little Red Riding Hood in the woods and asked, "Have you seen my smile?"

"No, but I'll help you look for it," she said.

He came upon Goldilocks and the three bears in their house and asked, "Have you seen my smile?"

"No, but we'll help you look for it," they said.

They all looked here, they all looked there, and they even looked deep down in the lake. Then they all fell in with a great big splash!

They all looked so funny standing in the water dripping wet that Sam laughed and laughed. He laughed so much that he found his smile, and they all lived happily ever after.

THE SAD GOBLIN

| **Right There** | Find the answers directly in the text. |

1. Find a word in the fairy tale to complete each sentence.

   a. Sam lost his _____.

   b. The three pigs _____ for Sam's smile.

   c. They all _____ into the lake.

2. Draw lines to match the following.

   a. Snow White   • three bears

   b. Goldilocks   • seven dwarfs

   c. Little Red Riding Hood   • the woods

| **Think and Search** | Think about what the text says. |

Read each sentence. Choose **Yes** or **No**.

1. Sam has lots of friends.   ☐ Yes ☐ No

2. Sam's friends wanted to help him.   ☐ Yes ☐ No

3. Sam's smile was in the lake.   ☐ Yes ☐ No

4. Sam wanted to be sad.   ☐ Yes ☐ No

5. Do you think Sam will keep his smile?   ☐ Yes ☐ No

   Why or why not? _____

   _____

THE SAD GOBLIN

On Your Own   Use what you know about the text and your own experience.

1. Draw a picture of someone who helps you.

2. My helper's name is _____.

3. My helper helps me _____

_____

_____.

THE SAD GOBLIN

Sensory Imaging

After reading the text on page 35, answer the following questions by using all five senses to create mental images of what you have read.

1. Write about Sam to complete the questions below.

   a. What/Who did Sam see?

     _____

     _____

   b. How did he feel?

     _____

   c. What do you think he could . . .

     touch? _____

     smell? _____

     hear? _____

2. Draw and write about what makes you laugh.

Making Connections

_____

_____

_____

_____

_____

_____

_____

_____

Genre: Play

READING FOCUS

- Analyzes and extracts information from a play to answer literal, inferential, and applied questions
- Scans for relevant information
- Makes connections based on prior knowledge and the text to predict feelings and reactions of characters

ANSWER KEY

Right There (Page 41)

1. a. Yes   b. No   c. No   d. Yes   e. Yes
2. sticks

Think and Search (Page 41)

1. frightened, scared, worried, sad, angry
2. Answers will vary. Possible answer(s): big, bad, mean, scary.

On Your Own (Page 42)

1. Drawings will vary.
2. Answers will vary. Possible answer(s): The brick house was too heavy to blow in.

Applying Strategies (Page 43)

1–5. Answers will vary.

EXTENSIONS

- Students can construct miniature houses using a variety of different materials.
- Students can read aloud and utilize Readers' Theater—using familiar text and different colored highlighter pens for each part.
- Collect, display, and read different versions of "The Three Little Pigs."

THE THREE LITTLE PIGS

Name _____

Read the play and answer the questions on the following pages.

Storyteller:	Once upon a time, there was a big, bad wolf who was very hungry. He went to the house made of straw and said to the first little pig:
Wolf:	Little pig, little pig, let me in.
First Little Pig:	No, not by the hair of my chinny-chin-chin. I will not let you in!
Wolf:	Then I'll huff and I'll puff, and I'll blow your house in.
Storyteller:	So he huffed and he puffed and he blew the house in. The first little pig ran to the second little pig's house made of sticks. The wolf followed him.
Wolf:	Little pig, little pig, let me in.
Second Little Pig:	No, not by the hair of my chinny-chin-chin. I will not let you in!
Wolf:	Then I'll huff and I'll puff, and I'll blow your house in.
Storyteller:	So he huffed and he puffed and he blew the house in. The two little pigs ran to the third little pig's house made of bricks. The wolf followed them.
Wolf:	Little pig, little pig, let me in.
Third Little Pig:	No, not by the hair of my chinny-chin-chin. I will not let you in!
Wolf:	Then I'll huff and I'll puff, and I'll blow your house in.
Storyteller:	So he huffed and he puffed and he huffed and he puffed, but he could not blow the house in.
Third Little Pig:	Let's get a big pot of hot water and put it in the chimney.
Storyteller:	The wolf climbed onto the roof and came down the chimney. He fell into the pot of water, and that was the end of the big, bad wolf.

THE THREE LITTLE PIGS

Right There   Find the answers directly in the text.

1. Read each sentence. Choose **Yes** or **No**.

   a. The wolf was hungry.   ☐ Yes ☐ No

   b. The wolf ate the pigs.   ☐ Yes ☐ No

   c. The pigs let the wolf in.   ☐ Yes ☐ No

   d. The wolf fell into the pot.   ☐ Yes ☐ No

   e. The wolf blew down the straw house. ☐ Yes ☐ No

2. What was the second little pig's house made of?

   _____

Think and Search   Think about what the text says.

1. How do you think the pigs were feeling? Place an **X** in the box next to each feeling that applies.

   ☐ frightened   ☐ surprised   ☐ glad

   ☐ scared   ☐ happy   ☐ angry

   ☐ sad   ☐ worried   ☐ silly

2. Write words to describe the wolf.

   _____

   _____

THE THREE LITTLE PIGS

On Your Own   Use what you know about the text and your own experience.

1. Draw the third little pig's house.

2. Why do you think the Wolf wasn't able to blow the third house in?

_____

_____

_____

THE THREE LITTLE PIGS

Two little pigs no longer have a house to live in. Draw a house that you think one of the pigs would like to build, then describe the house.

1. The house is made of _____.

2. The _____ little pig will live in it.

3. The house has _____ doors.

4. It has _____ windows.

5. I like the house because _____

_____.

Genre: Informational Visual Text—Book Cover

READING FOCUS

- Analyzes and extracts information from a visual text (a book cover) to answer literal, inferential, and applied questions
- Scans for relevant information
- Makes connections between a book cover viewed and one to be created
- Makes connections between a book cover and self

ANSWER KEY

Right There (Page 46)

1. a. Ian Celson
   b. Amy White
   c. *Justin and the Magic Apples*
2. a. Justin
   b. apples
   c. happy

Think and Search (Page 46)

1. a. Ian Celson — author
   b. Amy White — illustrator
2. a–c. Answers will vary.

On Your Own (Page 47)

Drawings and answers will vary.

Applying Strategies (Page 48)

1. Answers will vary.
2. Answers will vary.

EXTENSIONS

- Students can view different types of book covers including nonfiction and fiction books, comic books, newspapers, and magazines for comparison.
- Students can incorporate art to create patterned covers for class books or folders.

JUSTIN AND THE MAGIC APPLES

Name _____

Read the book cover and answer the questions on the following pages.

JUSTIN AND THE MAGIC APPLES

Right There   Find the answers directly in the text.

1. Copy words from the book cover to answer the following questions.

   a. Who wrote the book? _____

   b. Who drew the pictures for the book? _____

   c. What is the title of the book?

   _____

2. Place an **X** in the box next to the best answer.

   a. The name of the boy in the book is ☐ Justin   ☐ Ian.

   b. The magic fruits in the book are ☐ bananas   ☐ apples.

   c. Justin looks ☐ happy   ☐ sad   holding the magic apples.

Think and Search   Think about what the text says.

1. Draw lines to match the name to the person's correct title.

   a. Ian Celson   • illustrator

   b. Amy White   • author

2. Read each sentence and make a prediction. Choose **Yes** or **No**.

   a. Amy White is a good illustrator.   ☐ Yes   ☐ No

   b. The story is going to be interesting.   ☐ Yes   ☐ No

   c. Justin has done something good to   ☐ Yes   ☐ No
   get the magic apples.

JUSTIN AND THE MAGIC APPLES

On Your Own   Use what you know about the text and your own experience.

Draw a picture and write about what the magic apples will do for Justin.

_____

_____

_____

JUSTIN AND THE MAGIC APPLES

After reading the text on page 45, complete the following by making the connection between what you already know and the new information from the text.

1. Use the book cover on page 45 to help you make a book cover of your own. Check off the boxes when you have put in all the different parts.

☐ book title   ☐ cover illustration   ☐ name of author   ☐ name of illustrator

2. Write words telling what you would like magic apples to do for you.

_____

_____

Genre: Letter

READING FOCUS

- Analyzes and extracts information from a letter to answer literal, inferential, and applied questions
- Compares information in a text to own experiences

ANSWER KEY

Right There (Page 51)

1. a. Joel
   b. Nan and Pop
   c. a bike

2. a. black, red
   b. gray
   c. silver

3. jumped for joy.

4. a. Joel wrote a letter to Nan and Pop
   b. The bike has a kickstand and a bell.
   c. Joel rode his bike in the park.

Think and Search (Page 51)

1. Answers will vary. Possible answer(s): brother, friend, cousin.
2. Answers will vary. Possible answer(s): dog.

On Your Own (Page 52)

1. Drawings will vary.
2. Drawings will vary.

Applying Strategies (Page 53)

Answers will vary.

EXTENSIONS

- Students may enjoy having the following series of books read to them:
  - *The Jolly Postman (or Other People's Letters)* by Janet and Allan Ahlberg
  - *The Jolly Pocket Postman* by Janet and Allan Ahlberg
  - *The Jolly Christmas Postman* by Janet and Allan Ahlberg

THANK YOU

Name _____

Read the letter and answer the questions on the following pages.

Dear Nan and Pop,

I am writing to thank you both for my wonderful birthday present. When Mom and Dad told me that you wanted to buy me a bike, I jumped for joy! Now I don't have to beg Tyler to let me ride his.

They took me to the bike shop so I could choose. I picked out a red and black bike. It has a shiny silver bell and a kickstand so I can park it. Mom and Dad bought me a gray bike helmet as another birthday present. I have been riding along the bike path in the park while Mom or Dad take Bonnie for a walk on her leash.

I can't wait to come to the farm in the summertime. Tyler and I can both ride our bikes along the paths to the dam and the milking shed. See you soon!

Love,
   Joel

THANK YOU

1. Answer the following questions.

   a. Who wrote the letter? _____

   b. Who was the letter written to? _____

   c. What was the wonderful birthday present? _____

2. Find the colors in the letter to answer the following questions.

   a. What color was the bike? _____

   b. What color was the helmet? _____

   c. What color was the bell? _____

3. Write words from the letter to complete the sentence.

   When Joel found out he was getting a bike, he . . .

   _____

4. Match the beginning of each sentence to its ending.

   a. Joel wrote a letter to   • a kickstand and bell.

   b. The bike has   • in the park.

   c. Joel rode his bike   • Nan and Pop.

Answer the following questions.

1. Who do you think Tyler is?

   _____

2. What kind of pet do you think Bonnie is?

   _____

THANK YOU

Use what you know about the text and your own experience.

1. Draw three things you could see on a farm.

2. Draw three presents someone your age would like for his/her birthday.

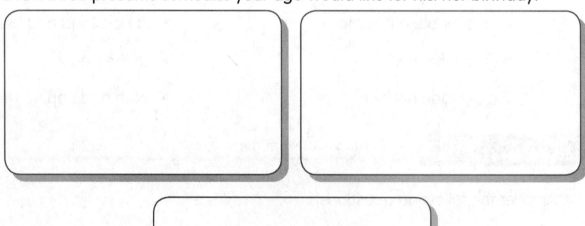

THANK YOU

Comparing

Use the text on page 50 to complete the activity. Complete the empty boxes with words or pictures about your bike or one you would like to own.

	Joel's Bike	Your Bike
This is a picture of the bike.		
What color is it?	red and black	
Describe the bell if it has one.	shiny and silver	
Does it have a kickstand?	Yes	
What does the bike helmet look like?	It is gray.	
Where could the bike be ridden?	on the bike path at the park

along the paths at the farm | |

Genre: Science Fiction

READING FOCUS

- Analyzes and extracts information from a science-fiction text to answer literal, inferential, and applied questions
- Compares information in a text to own experiences

ANSWER KEY

Right There (Page 56)

1. a. The family lived on <u>Moon</u> Street.

   b. John bought Russell at the <u>robot</u> shop.

   c. The <u>repairman</u> appeared in the <u>teleporter</u>.

Think and Search (Page 56)

1. John — dad

2. Sarah — mom

3. Alex — older brother

4. Daniel — younger brother

On Your Own (Page 57)

1. Drawings/answers will vary.

2. Drawings and answers will vary.

Applying Strategies (Page 58)

Answers will vary.

EXTENSIONS

- Other titles that students may enjoy having read to them include the following:
  - *Jed and the Space Bandits* by Jean and Claudio Marzollo
  - *Commander Toad in Space* by Jane Yolen
  - *Aliens for Breakfast* by Jonathon Etra

Name _____

Read the science-fiction story and answer the questions on the following pages.

Russell was a very good robot. He lived with his family—John, Sarah, Alex, and Daniel—in a space pod on Moon Street. Alex was the oldest child. He was 13 years old, and Daniel was 6. Russell was Daniel's best friend. Alex didn't like to play with Daniel very much, so John bought Russell at the robot shop to look after Daniel. They played "Fly and Seek," "Robot Rescue," and "Galaxy Wars."

One day when Russell and Daniel were playing, there was a loud *bang!* and smoke started to come from Russell's metal chest. He came to a sudden stop. Daniel called to his mom. She called the emergency robot service number. In the blink of a star, the repairman appeared in the teleporter. He fixed Russell, and soon Daniel and Russell were playing happily together.

RUSSELL THE ROBOT AND HIS BEST BUDDY

Right There   Find the answers directly in the text.

1. Fill in the blanks with words from the story.

a. The family lived on _____ Street.

b. John bought Russell at the _____ shop.

c. The _____ appeared in the _____.

Think and Search   Think about what the text says.

Match the name to the person.

1. John

2. Sarah

3. Alex

4. Daniel

• younger brother

• older brother

• mom

• dad

RUSSELL THE ROBOT AND HIS BEST BUDDY

On Your Own   Use what you know about the text and your own experience.

1. Draw or write the names of five mechanical things in your house.

2. Draw a pet robot you would like to have. Write about what you would like your pet robot to do.

_____

_____

_____

_____

_____

_____

_____

RUSSELL THE ROBOT AND HIS BEST BUDDY

Comparing

Use the text on page 55 to make comparisons. Complete the empty boxes using words or pictures.

Daniel's family	Your family
Family members John (dad) Sarah (mom) Alex (big brother) Russell (the robot)	Family members
Daniel's best friend Russell (the robot)	Your best friend
Games played with friends "Fly and Seek" "Robot Rescue" "Galaxy Wars"	Games played with friends
Home space pod on Moon Street	Home
Repairmen who visit robot repairman	Repairmen who visit

Genre: Poetry

READING FOCUS

- Analyzes and extracts information from an action rhyme to answer literal, inferential, and applied questions
- Uses sensory imaging to create mental images of the actions in a poem

ANSWER KEY

Right There (Page 61)

1. The girl hugs her kitten tight.
2. a. frown
   b. bite
   c. bad
   d. peep
3. a. True
   b. True
   c. False

Think and Search (Page 61)

1. Yes
2. No
3. No
4. No

On Your Own (Page 62)

Drawings and answers will vary.

Applying Strategies (Page 63)

Answers will vary.

EXTENSIONS

- Students can learn the poem and add their own actions.
- Students can perform other action rhymes such as "Ten Little Fingers," "Two Old Tortoises," and action songs, such as "Heads, Shoulders, Knees, and Toes."

Name _____

Read the poem and answer the questions on the following pages.

When I see a laughing clown,

My mouth goes up. I do not frown.

When I hug my kitten tight,

She turns her head and starts to bite.

When Mom scolds and Dad gets mad,

The tears run down, 'cause I've been bad,

But when my head goes down to sleep,

I close my eyes and do not peep.

ACTION RHYME

Right There   Find the answers directly in the text.

1. What does the girl do to her kitten?

   _____

2. Copy a word from the poem that rhymes with:

   a. clown _____

   b. tight _____

   c. mad _____

   d. sleep _____

3. Read each sentence. Decide if each statement is **True** or **False**.

   a. The kitten bites when it is hugged too tightly.   ❑ True   ❑ False

   b. The girl in the poem is bad sometimes.   ❑ True   ❑ False

   c. The girl smiles when her mom scolds her.   ❑ True   ❑ False

Think and Search   Think about what the text says.

Read each sentence. Choose **Yes** or **No**.

1. Clowns make the girl happy.   ❑ Yes   ❑ No

2. The kitten likes being hugged very tightly.   ❑ Yes   ❑ No

3. The girl is treated unfairly by her
   mom and dad.   ❑ Yes   ❑ No

4. The girl sleeps poorly at night.   ❑ Yes   ❑ No

ACTION RHYME

On Your Own   Use what you know about the text and your own experience.

Draw four things that children can do. Write words to complete each sentence.

I CAN . . .

_____.

I CAN . . .

_____.

I CAN . . .

_____.

I CAN . . .

_____.

ACTION RHYME

Sensory Imaging

Write words or draw pictures to complete the boxes about the actions in the poem.

a. When I see a laughing clown, I . . .	**b.** When I hug a kitten, I . . .	**c.** When Mom scolds and Dad gets mad, I . . .	**d.** When I am going to sleep, I . . .
touch . . .	touch . . .	touch . . .	touch . . .
hear . . .	hear . . .	hear . . .	hear . . .
smell . . .	smell . . .	smell . . .	smell . . .
see . . .	see . . .	see . . .	see . . .

Genre: Fantasy

READING FOCUS

- Analyzes and extracts information from a fantasy text to answer literal, inferential, and applied questions

- Determines the most important aspects of main characters

ANSWER KEY

Right There (Page 66)

1. a. William

   b. Wanda

   c. It was her birthday.

   d. gift box of stars/sparkles

2. a. sun   b. sparkles   c. trees   d. wonderful

Think and Search (Page 66)

1. Yes   2. Yes   3. No   4. Yes

On Your Own (Page 67)

Drawings and answers will vary.

Applying Strategies (Page 68)

William the Wizard
    Drawings and answers will vary. Possible answer(s):
    I am . . . a wizard, Wanda's best friend.
    I like . . . to make friends happy, to give special gifts.
    I like my friend Wanda because . . . she is nice, she is fun.

Wanda the Witch
    Drawings and answers will vary. Possible answer(s):
    I am . . . a witch, William's best friend.
    I like . . . sparkly gifts, having birthday parties.
    I like my friend William because . . . he is nice, he is thoughtful, he makes me smile.

EXTENSIONS

- Other titles that students may enjoy having read to them include the following:
  - *Winnie the Witch* by Korky Paul and Valerie Thomas
  - *Room on the Broom* by Julia Donaldson
  - *The Spiffiest Giant in Town* by Julia Donaldson
  - *Big Pumpkin* by Erica Silverman

Name _____

Read the fantasy story and answer the questions on the following pages.

William the wizard sat on his bed and began to think.

In two days, it was going to be his best friend and neighbor, Wanda's, birthday. Wanda was a very lucky witch. Her parents loved her very much, and she had all the toys she wanted. William wanted to give her a special gift that no one else would give her. He thought and thought. At last, he had an idea!

The day of Wanda's party arrived. William had a big grin on his face when he gave Wanda her gift box.

"You'll have to wait until the sun goes down to open your present!" he said.

When all the guests had gone home, William watched from his bedroom window as the sun went down. He could see Wanda in her bedroom looking at the box.

Suddenly, the box burst open! Sparkles of rainbow-colored dust flew into the air, circled Wanda's head, and fell onto the trees outside Wanda's window. They glowed and twinkled in the darkness.

"What a wonderful gift!" she said. "The best one I've ever had! Now I have my own stars to light up the night right outside my bedroom window!"

William just smiled to himself.

THE WONDERFUL BIRTHDAY GIFT

Right There   Find the answers directly in the text.

1. Copy words from the story to answer the following questions.

   a. What was the wizard's name? _____

   b. What was the name of his best friend? _____

   c. Why was Wanda having a party? _____

   d. What did William give Wanda? _____

2. Choose a word from the word bank to complete the sentences.

sparkles	wonderful	sun	trees

   a. Wanda had to wait until the _____ went down to open her present.

   b. The box was filled with _____.

   c. The sparkles landed on the _____ outside Wanda's window.

   d. Wanda thought the gift was _____.

Think and Search   Think about what the text says.

Read each sentence. Choose **Yes** or **No**.

1. William liked Wanda. ☐ Yes ☐ No

2. William wanted to give Wanda a nice present because she was his best friend. ☐ Yes ☐ No

3. Wanda was told not to open her gift until the sun went down because it was not as good as the other gifts. ☐ Yes ☐ No

4. William was happy that Wanda liked her gift. ☐ Yes ☐ No

THE WONDERFUL BIRTHDAY GIFT

On Your Own   Use what you know about the text and your own experience.

Draw and write about a special gift you have been given.

_____

_____

_____

THE WONDERFUL BIRTHDAY GIFT

Determining Importance

Use the text on page 65 to complete the questions. Draw a picture and write words to tell about William and Wanda.

William the Wizard

I am . . .

_____

_____.

I like . . .

_____

_____.

I like my friend Wanda because . . .

_____

_____.

Wanda the Witch

I am . . .

_____

_____.

I like . . .

_____

_____.

I like my friend William because . . .

_____

_____

Genre: Myth

READING FOCUS

- Analyzes and extracts information from a myth to answer literal, inferential, and applied questions
- Determines the importance of events in a myth to summarize and retell the story

ANSWER KEY

Right There (Page 71)

1. a. golden   b. seaweed   c. cave at the bottom of the sea

2. a. The mermaid sang about a golden light.

   b. Clytie swam to the surface to see the golden light.

   c. The golden light was the Sun.

3. a. petals   b. roots   c. leaves

Think and Search (Page 71)

1. a. Yes   b. No   c. No

2. Answers will vary. Possible answer(s): She loved it because she was able to face the Sun all day long.

On Your Own (Page 72)

Picture of the sunflower facing the Sun

Applying Strategies (Page 73)

Drawings and answers will vary. Possible answer(s):

Beginning: Clytie lived in a cave at the bottom of the sea. (picture of Clytie living in an underwater cave)

Middle: Clytie heard a mermaid singing about the golden light. (picture of a mermaid singing)

Middle: Clytie swam to the surface and saw the Sun. (picture of Clytie sitting on a rock, looking at the Sun)

Ending: Clytie turned into a sunflower. (picture of Clytie as a sunflower, facing the Sun)

EXTENSIONS

- Books containing myths suitable for this age group are:
  - *Greek Myths for Young Children* by Heather Amery
  - *15 Greek Myth Mini-Books* by Danielle Blood
  - *Classic Myths to Read Aloud* by William F. Russell

THE SUNFLOWER

Name _____

Read the myth and answer the questions on the following pages.

Once upon a time, there was a beautiful nymph named Clytie. She lived in a cave at the bottom of the sea. Clytie had long golden hair. She wore a green gown made of seaweed.

One day, Clytie heard a mermaid singing. Her song was about a golden light that shone above the water. Clytie longed to see this wonderful light.

She decided to swim to the surface and climb onto a rock. There she saw the wonderful golden light. It was the Sun! She sat looking at the Sun all that day, the next day, and the next.

At last, she looked down into the water. She saw that her hair had become yellow petals. Her green gown had become leaves, and her tiny feet had become roots. Clytie had become a sunflower!

If you look closely at a sunflower, you will see that it turns its face to follow the Sun as it moves across the sky.

THE SUNFLOWER

Right There   Find the answers directly in the text.

1. Write words from the story to answer the questions.

   a. What color was Clytie's hair? _____

   b. What was her gown made of? _____

   c. Where did she live? _____

2. Match the beginning of the sentence to its ending.

   a. The mermaid sang about   • was the Sun.

   b. Clytie swam to the surface   • a golden light.

   c. The golden light   • to see the golden light.

3. Clytie became a sunflower. Write what each part of her turned into.

   a. Her hair turned into _____.

   b. Her feet turned into _____.

   c. Her gown turned into _____.

Think and Search   Think about what the text says.

1. Read each sentence. Choose **Yes** or **No**.

   a. Clytie looked at the Sun for three days.   ☐ Yes ☐ No

   b. A sunflower is an animal.   ☐ Yes ☐ No

   c. Clytie had been to the surface lots of times. ☐ Yes ☐ No

2. How do you think Clytie felt about turning into a sunflower?

   _____

   _____

THE SUNFLOWER

On Your Own   Use what you know about the text and your own experience.

What is wrong with this picture? Draw how it should look
in the blank box. Write a sentence about your picture.

_____

_____

_____

_____

72

THE SUNFLOWER

Use the text on page 70 to complete the following activity. Draw a picture and write words in each box to show what happened in each part of the story.

Beginning

Middle

Middle

Ending

Retell the story to a friend.

Genre: Fable

READING FOCUS

- Analyzes and extracts information from a fable to answer literal, inferential, and applied questions
- Scans a text to locate words

ANSWER KEY

Right There (Page 76)

1. a. False   b. False   c. True   d. False   e. True
2. a. lake   b. his home   c. day   d. black   e. eat

Think and Search (Page 76)

1. white feathers
2. He thought the swan was beautiful.
3. He wanted to be close to the lake where the swan lived.
4. He thought the water would turn his feathers white and he would be beautiful like the swan.

On Your Own (Page 77)

1. Drawings will vary.
2. Answer will vary. Possible answer(s): eat fruits and vegetables, drink plenty of water, get enough sleep, exercise.

Applying Strategies (Page 78)

1. a. white   b. black   c. feathers   d. beautiful

   e. home   f. black, white   g. eat
2. Answers will vary. Possible answer(s): s—swan   w—washing   b—black

---

EXTENSIONS

- Other fables by Aesop, which may be read to students, include the following:
  - "The Ant and the Grasshopper"
  - "The Tortoise and the Hare"
  - "The Lion and the Mouse"
  - "The Fox and the Grapes"
- Students may discuss the moral of the fables.

Name _____

Read the fable and answer the questions on the following pages.

A black raven saw a beautiful white swan washing her feathers in the water while she was swimming. The raven wanted to be as beautiful as the swan.

The raven left his home and went to live near the lake where the swan lived. He cleaned his feathers every day in the water, but his feathers did not change from black to white. He spent so much time trying to make himself beautiful that he did not eat and soon perished.

THE RAVEN AND THE SWAN

Right There   Find the answers directly in the text.

1. Read each sentence. Decide if each statement is **True** or **False**.

   a. The raven was white.   ☐ True   ☐ False

   b. The swan was black.   ☐ True   ☐ False

   c. The swan was beautiful.   ☐ True   ☐ False

   d. The raven thought the swan was ugly.   ☐ True   ☐ False

   e. The raven perished.   ☐ True   ☐ False

2. Write words from the fable to complete the sentences.

   a. The swan lived near the _____.

   b. The raven left _____.

   c. The raven washed his feathers every _____.

   d. The raven's feathers stayed _____.

   e. The raven did not _____.

Think and Search   Think about what the text says.

Write words to answer the questions.

   1. What color feathers did the raven consider beautiful?

   _____

   2. Why did the raven want to be like the swan?

   _____

   3. Why did the raven leave his own home?

   _____

   4. What did the raven think the water would do to his feathers?

   _____

THE RAVEN AND THE SWAN

On Your Own   Use what you know about the text and your own experience.

1. Draw two birds that look very different but are both still beautiful. If you can, label each with its name.

2. The raven in the story was so busy trying to make himself beautiful that he didn't take good care of himself. List three ways you take care of yourself.

- _____

  _____

- _____

  _____

- _____

  _____

THE RAVEN AND THE SWAN

Scanning

Scan the text on page 75 and locate specific details to help you answer the questions.

1. Copy words from the fable to finish the sentences.

   a. The swan had _____ feathers.

   b. The raven had _____ feathers.

   c. The swan was washing her _____ in the water.

   d. The raven wanted to be as _____ as the swan.

   e. The raven left his _____.

   f. The raven's feathers did not change from _____ to _____.

   g. The raven did not _____ so he perished.

2. Write three different words from the fable that begin with the sound in each box.

s	w
_____	_____

b
_____

READING FOCUS

- Analyzes and extracts information from a folktale to answer literal, inferential, and applied questions
- Scans text to identify relevant events
- Uses synthesis to recall information and order details to sequence a story

---

ANSWER KEY

Right There (Page 81)

1. The bear's tail froze.
2. long, bushy
3. a. fox, fish   b. pull, jerk   c. tail, frozen

Think and Search (Page 81)

1. Yes   2. Yes   3. No   4. No

On Your Own (Page 82)

Drawings and answers will vary.

Applying Strategies (Page 83)

1. The fox stole some fish.
2. The fox met the bear.
3. The fox told the bear how to catch a fish.
4. The bear cut a hole in the ice.
5. The bear stuck his long tail in the hole.
6. The bear's tail had snapped off!

EXTENSIONS

- Students may enjoy listening to other folktales concerning how or why something is so. Some titles are:
  - "How the Kangaroo Got Its Pouch"
  - "How the Porcupine Got Its Quills"
  - "Why the Bat Has No Friends"
  - "How the Sky Came to Be"

- The *Just So Stories for Little Children* are a collection written by Rudyard Kipling. Titles include the following:
  - "How the Whale Got Its Throat"
  - "How the Leopard Got Its Spots"
  - "How the Rhinoceros Got Its Skin"
  - "How the Alphabet Was Made"

WHY THE BEAR HAS A STUMPY TAIL

Name _____

Read the folktale and answer the questions on the following pages.

Long ago, the bear had a long, bushy tail, much like a fox's tail. One day, the bear met a fox. The fox had some fish he had stolen.

"Where did you get the fish?" asked the bear.

"I caught them," said the fox.

"How did you catch them?" asked the bear.

"Oh, it's easy. Just cut a hole in the ice and stick your long tail in the water. Hold it there for as long as you can. The fish will bite your tail, so hold on. Then, pull up your tail with a strong jerk."

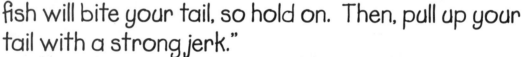

So the bear did what the fox said. He held his tail down a long, long time in the cold, cold water. His tail became frozen. At last, he pulled his tail up. It snapped off!

And that is why the bear has a stumpy tail.

WHY THE BEAR HAS A STUMPY TAIL

Right There   Find the answers directly in the text.

1. Which event happened in the story?

   ❏ The fox's tail snapped off.

   ❏ The bear caught a fish.

   ❏ The bear's tail froze.

2. Place an **X** in the box next to the words that describe what the bear's tail looked like long ago.

   ❏ long   ❏ stumpy   ❏ short   ❏ bushy   ❏ little

3. Complete the sentences by copying words from the story.

   a. The bear asked the _____ where he got

   the _____.

   b. The fox told the bear to _____ up his tail

   with a strong _____.

   c. The bear held his _____ in the water for

   so long that it became _____.

Think and Search   Think about what the text says.

Read each sentence. Choose **Yes** or **No**.

   1. The fox told lies.   ❏ Yes   ❏ No

   2. The bear believed the fox.   ❏ Yes   ❏ No

   3. The bear caught some fish.   ❏ Yes   ❏ No

   4. The fox helped the bear pull his tail up.   ❏ Yes   ❏ No

WHY THE BEAR HAS A STUMPY TAIL

On Your Own   Use what you know about the text and your own experience.

Draw another way the bear could have caught some fish.

_____

_____

_____

WHY THE BEAR HAS A STUMPY TAIL

Sequencing

Use the text on page 80 to complete the following activity. Draw the missing pictures from the story. Color and cut out the pictures, and put them in the correct order to tell the story.

The bear cut a hole in the ice.

The bear stuck his long tail in the hole.

The fox met the bear.

The bear's tail had snapped off!

The fox told the bear how to catch a fish.

The fox stole some fish.

Genre: Humor

READING FOCUS

- Analyzes and extracts information from a humorous poem to answer literal, inferential, and applied questions
- Synthezises and completes details about the events in a humorous poem to show order

ANSWER KEY

Right There (Page 86)

1. Mr. Grumble, Tilly Tidy-up, cat, dog, mouse
2. a. Tilly made cake, buns, and drinks.
   b. Tilly put the cat and dog safely out of sight.
   c. The cat and dog chased the mouse.
   d. The food and dishes fell in a heap.

Think and Search (Page 86)

1. a. False   b. True   c. False
2. Answers will vary. Possible answer(s): fun, chaotic, messy, loud.

On Your Own (Page 87)

Drawings and answers will vary.

Applying Strategies (Page 88)

1. Tilly cleans up.
2. Tilly puts out the food and drinks.
3. Tilly puts the cat and dog away.
4. The guests eat their food.
5. The cat and dog chase the mouse around the table.
6. The food and dishes fall into a heap.
7. The guests laugh and eat mushy buns.

EXTENSIONS

- Other titles that students may enjoy having read to them include the following:
  - *Olivia* by Ian Falconer
  - *Giraffes Can't Dance* by Giles Andrede and Guy Parker Rees
  - *The Berenstein Bears* stories by Stan and Jan Berenstein
- Read limericks and "knock, knock" jokes to the students and allow them to tell or write some of their own.

Name _____

Read the humorous poem and answer the questions on the following pages.

Tilly Tidy-up was in a tizzy.

The house was so clean that Tilly was dizzy.

The food was ready. The drinks were poured.

Soon the guests would knock at the door.

The cat and dog, her heart's delight,

Were safely placed out of sight.

None of her guests would hear a peep,

As they ate their cake and rested their feet.

The time was passing happily.

The guests were chatting noisily.

When soon was heard a squeaking sound,

And chaos then was all around.

The mouse sped in—the cat behind.

The dog came next in record time.

Round and round the tabletop

The animals ran and did not stop.

Food and dishes fell in a heap.

All the guests began to shriek.

Mr. Grumble, loud and round,

Began to laugh, and Tilly soon found . . .

That all were having so much fun,

They even ate the mushy buns.

TILLY TIDY-UP

Right There   Find the answers directly in the text.

1. Place an **X** in the box next to the characters in the poem.

❏ Mr. Grumble   ❏ mouse   ❏ boy

❏ Tilly Tidy-up   ❏ bird   ❏ cat

❏ dog   ❏ girl

2. Match the beginning of the sentence to its ending.

a. Tilly made   • safely out of sight.

b. Tilly put the cat and dog   • cake, buns, and drinks.

c. The cat and dog chased   • in a heap.

d. The food and dishes fell   • the mouse.

Think and Search   Think about what the text says.

1. Read each sentence. Decide if each statement is **True** or **False**.

a. Tilly did not love her cat and dog.   ❏ True ❏ False

b. The pets were put away so that they   ❏ True ❏ False
would not disturb the guests.

c. Mr. Grumble was a thin man.   ❏ True ❏ False

2. List three words to describe the party.

• _____

• _____

• _____

TILLY TIDY-UP

On Your Own   Use what you know about the text and your own experience.

Draw a picture and write about a time when your pet, or a pet you know, got into mischief.

_____

_____

_____

TILLY TIDY-UP

Sequencing

Use the text on page 85 to complete the following activity. Write numbers 1 to 7 next to each event to show the order in which they happened. Then, draw pictures to match the sentences.

Tilly puts out the food and drinks.

Tilly cleans up.

Tilly puts the cat and dog away.

The guests eat their food.

The food and dishes fall into a heap.

The cat and dog chase the mouse around the table.

The guests laugh and eat mushy buns.

Genre: Procedure

READING FOCUS

- Analyzes and extracts information from a procedure to answer literal, inferential, and applied questions
- Scans text to identify relevant events
- Uses synthesis to recall information and order details to sequence a procedure

ANSWER KEY

Right There (Page 91)

1. a. ready-made pizza crust

   b. pizza sauce

   c. grated cheese

2. tomato, onion, mushroom

3. a. The pizza is placed on an oven tray.

   b. The ham, bell pepper, and pineapple are chopped into pieces.

   c. The cheese is grated.

Think and Search (Page 91)

1. pineapple, tomato, onion, bell pepper   2. oven mitts

On Your Own (Page 92)

1–2. Answers and drawings will vary.

Applying Strategies (Page 93)

1. Spread pizza sauce over the ready-made pizza crust.

2. Sprinkle with grated cheese.

3. Top with sliced tomato, onion, bell pepper, and mushroom.

4. Add chopped ham and pineapple pieces.

5. Place pizza on an oven tray.

6. Bake in a hot oven until the cheese is melted and bubbly.

EXTENSIONS

- Students can draw and write simple steps to explain how to make a milkshake, a sandwich, a fruit salad, or a dish of their own choice for others to sequence.
- Students can make the pizza as directed or the one they drew the ingredients for in question #2 on page 92. After tasting, they could rate it from 1 to 5 and suggest improvements if necessary.

Name _____

Read the procedure and answer the questions on the following pages.

You will need:

- oven tray
- pizza sauce
- ready-made pizza crust
- grated cheese
- pineapple pieces

- sliced tomato
- sliced onion
- chopped bell pepper
- sliced mushroom
- chopped ham

Directions:

1. Spread pizza sauce over the ready-made pizza crust.

2. Sprinkle with grated cheese.

3. Top with sliced tomato, onion, bell pepper, and mushroom.

4. Add chopped ham and pineapple pieces.

5. Place pizza on an oven tray.

6. With an adult's help, bake in a hot oven until the cheese is melted and bubbly.

HOW TO MAKE A PIZZA

Right There   Find the answers directly in the text.

Answer the following questions.

1. Choose words from the procedure.

    a. What kind of crust was used? _____

    b. What was spread on the crust? _____

    c. What was sprinkled on the pizza? _____

2. List all the items that were sliced.

    _____

3. Match each sentence beginning to its ending.

    a. The pizza is placed   • is grated.

    b. The ham, bell pepper,   • on an oven tray.
    and pineapple

    c. The cheese   • are chopped into pieces.

Think and Search   Think about what the text says.

1. List four fruits or vegetables that were put on the pizza.

    • _____   • _____

    • _____   • _____

2. What would you need to use to pull the pizza out of the oven?

    _____

HOW TO MAKE A PIZZA

On Your Own   Use what you know about the text and your own experience.

1. Place an **X** in the box next to the things you would like on a pizza. Add any others.

☐ cheese   ☐ onion   ☐ pizza sauce   ☐ pineapple

☐ tomato   ☐ ham   ☐ mushroom   ☐ _____

2. Draw what you would like to put on a pizza.

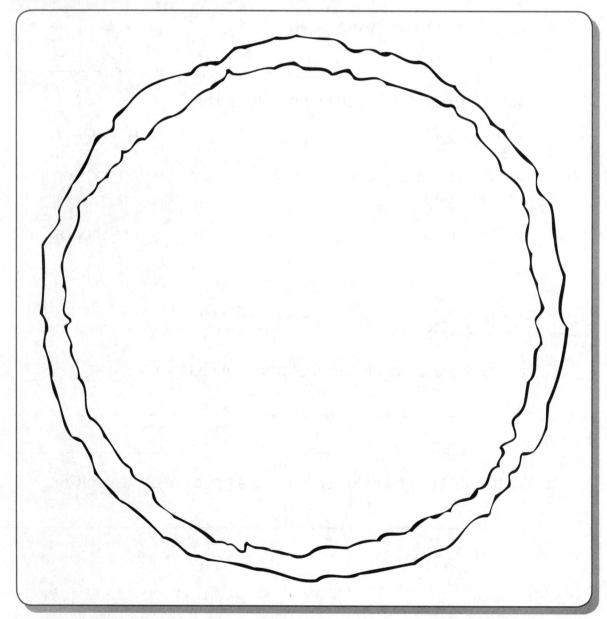

HOW TO MAKE A PIZZA

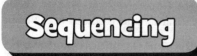

Draw the missing pictures and write the missing sentences about how to make a pizza. Color and cut them out, and put them in the correct order. Use the procedure on page 90 to help you.

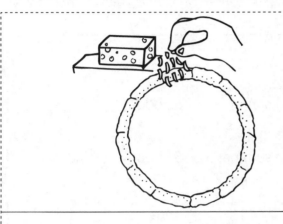

Top with sliced tomato, onion, bell pepper, and mushroom.

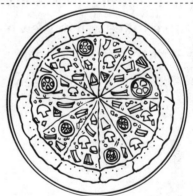

With an adult's help, bake in a hot oven until the cheese is melted and bubbly.

Spread pizza sauce over the ready-made pizza crust.

Teacher Information

Genre: Cartoon—
Visual Text

READING FOCUS

- Analyzes and extracts information from a cartoon to answer literal, inferential, and applied questions
- Summarizes information in a cartoon by drawing a life-cycle diagram

---

ANSWER KEY

Right There (Page 96)

  1. Bill, Ben   2. fall   3. winter   4. spring   5. odd

Think and Search (Page 96)

  1. deciduous   2. evergreen   3. cold   4. summer   5. happy

On Your Own (Page 97)

  Drawings and answers will vary.

Applying Strategies (Page 98)

  Summer—Picture of tree full of leaves

  Fall—Picture of tree with very few multi-colored leaves left on the branches

  Winter—Picture of tree with bare branches

  Spring—Picture of tree with green leaves starting to grow back

---

EXTENSIONS

- Other titles about life cycles that students may enjoy reading include the following:
  - *The Very Hungry Caterpillar* by Eric Carle
  - *Alfie's Long Winter* by Greg McEvoy
  - *Squiggly Wiggly's Surprise* by Arnold Shapiro
  - *A Butterfly Is Born* by Melvin Berger
- Read nonfiction books about seasons and the life cycle of various animals and plants.

CARTOON

Name _____

Read the cartoon and answer the questions on the following pages.

CARTOON

Right There	Find the answers directly in the text.

Copy words from the cartoon on page 95 to answer the following questions.

1. What are the names of the two trees?

_____ and _____

2. When did Ben start to lose his leaves? _____

3. When did Ben have bare branches? _____

4. When did Ben start to grow new leaves? _____

5. How did Bill think Ben looked without leaves? _____

Think and Search	Think about what the text says.

Place an **X** in the box next to the best answer.

1. Ben is a/an ❏ **evergreen** ❏ **deciduous** tree.

2. Bill is a/an ❏ **deciduous** ❏ **evergreen** tree.

3. In winter, the weather is most likely ❏ **cold** ❏ **hot**.

4. Ben has all his leaves back by ❏ **spring** ❏ **summer**.

5. Bill was ❏ **happy** ❏ **sad** that he had leaves all year round.

CARTOON

Choose an animal or plant, and draw pictures and write about its life cycle.

_____

_____

_____

CARTOON

Summarizing

Use the cartoon on page 95 to complete a drawing of the life cycle of a deciduous tree.

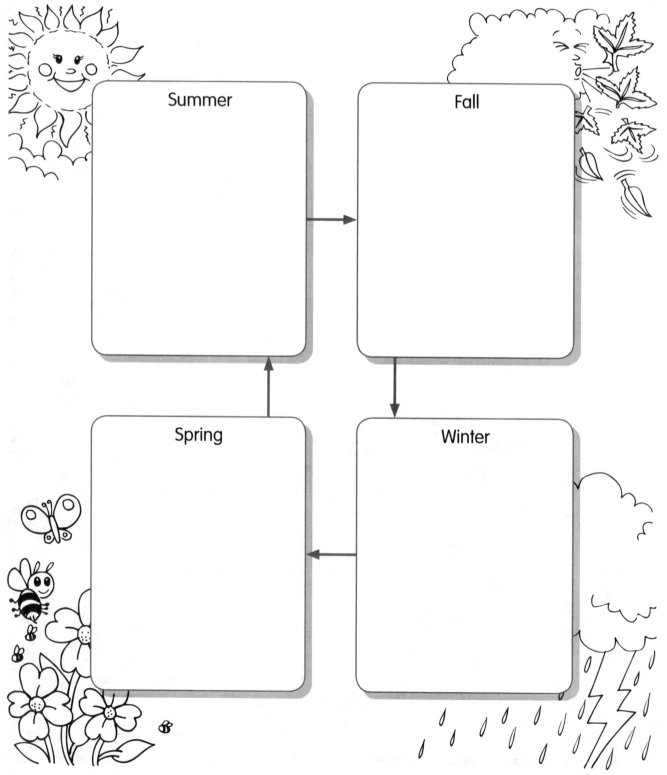

Summer

Fall

Spring

Winter

READING FOCUS

- Analyzes and extracts information from a report to answer literal, inferential, and applied questions
- Scans text to determine important information
- Summarizes text by recording keywords and phrases

ANSWER KEY

Right There (Page 101)

1. The <u>elephant</u> is the <u>largest</u> animal that <u>lives</u> on land.

2. a. 4   b. 2   c. 2   d. 1

3. a. No   b. No   c. Yes   d. Yes

Think and Search (Page 101)

1. fruit

2. Answers will vary. Possible answer(s): to keep cool on a hot day.

On Your Own (Page 102)

1. a. lamb   b. puppy   c. calf   d. kitten

2. Drawings will vary.

Applying Strategies (Page 103)

a. ears—large   b. legs and feet—strong   c. trunk—long

d. skin—gray and wrinkled   e. tusks—pointy and white   f. tail—thin

g. grass, leaves, bark, fruit h. Drawings will vary.   i. Answers will vary.

EXTENSIONS

- Students may enjoy having books about animal facts read to them. Some suggested titles include the following:
  - *Animal Books for Young Children* published by Acorn Naturalists
  - *The Faces of Nature* series by Mymi Doinet
  - *Wild, Wild World* series by Tanya Lee Stone

Name _____

Read the report and answer the questions on the following pages.

The elephant is the largest animal that lives on land. It has four strong legs and feet that are almost round. Its skin is gray and wrinkled. The elephant has two very large ears. It has a long trunk and two pointy white tusks. Its tail is thin.

The elephant likes to live in a group. It eats grass, leaves, bark, and fruit. The elephant uses its trunk to put food and water into its mouth. It also uses its trunk to spray water over its back.

A baby elephant is called a calf. An elephant can live for about 65 years.

THE ELEPHANT

Right There   Find the answers directly in the text.

1. Choose words from the word bank to fill in the missing words.

largest	lives	elephant

The _____ is the _____ animal

that _____ on land.

2. Write the correct number.

   a. How many legs does an elephant have?   _____

   b. How many tusks does an elephant have?   _____

   c. How many ears does an elephant have?   _____

   d. How many tails does an elephant have?   _____

3. Read each sentence. Choose **Yes** or **No**.

   a. An elephant has smooth skin.   ☐ Yes   ☐ No

   b. A baby elephant is a cub.   ☐ Yes   ☐ No

   c. An elephant likes to live in a group. ☐ Yes   ☐ No

   d. An elephant can live for about 65 years. ☐ Yes   ☐ No

Think and Search   Think about what the text says.

1. What food do you eat that an elephant also likes to eat?

   _____

2. Why do you think an elephant sprays water over its back?

   _____

THE ELEPHANT

On Your Own   Use what you know about the text and your own experience.

1. Finish the sentence with a word from the box.

puppy	calf	kitten	lamb

a. A baby sheep is called a _____.

b. A baby dog is called a _____.

c. A baby cow is called a _____.

d. A baby cat is called a _____.

2. Draw two animals that are almost as large as an elephant.

Name _____

THE ELEPHANT

Scanning

Scan the text on page 100 to complete the following activity. Find words in the report about the elephant to complete the chart.

The Elephant

What does it look like?

a. ears	**b.** legs and feet
c. trunk	**d.** skin
e. tusks	**f.** tail

g. What does it eat?

h. Draw something it likes to do.

i. Provide an interesting fact.

Genre: Adventure

READING FOCUS

- Analyzes and extracts information from an adventure story to answer literal, inferential, and applied question
- Scans text to identify relevant events
- Completes a story map to summarize main events

ANSWER KEY

Right There (Page 106)

1. a. My granddad lives next to the wild woods.

   b. We like to take a walk in the woods.

   c. I hold on to his hand.

2. a. 2   b. 10   c. 10

3. a. Yes   b. No   c. No   d. No

Think and Search (Page 106)

1. the frog

2. Answers will vary. Possible answer(s): They were scared because they were unsure of where the sounds were coming from.

On Your Own (Page 107)

1. Drawings will vary.

2. Drawings will vary.

Applying Strategies (Page 108)

Check drawings for accuracy.

EXTENSIONS

- Students can retell the story, adding a different character, deleting a character, or changing the ending.
- Students can create a story map. Fairy tales, such as "The Three Little Pigs," "Goldilocks and the Three Bears," "The Gingerbread Man," and "Little Red Riding Hood," are suitable for story-map activities. Another popular title ideal for a story map is *Rosie's Walk* by Pat Hutchkins.

A WALK IN THE WOODS

Name _____

Read the adventure and answer the questions on the following pages.

My granddad lives next to the wild woods. I hold on to his hand when we take a walk in the woods. What will happen this time?

We walk along the winding path. We see a nest in a tree. We tiptoe past two baby birds. We climb over a little log. We count ten tiny mushrooms on the grass. We look at a busy bee. We say hello to a wriggling worm. We run past a speedy spider. We step over a big puddle. We find ten tadpoles in a pond. Then . . .

CROAK! QUACK! WHAT IS THAT?

We hold hands tightly.

Oh! It's just a friendly frog and a diving duck.

We say goodbye. We walk back along the winding path.

A WALK IN THE WOODS

Right There   Find the answers directly in the text.

1. Match each sentence beginning to its ending.

   a. My granddad lives   • to his hand.

   b. We like to take a   • next to the wild woods.

   c. I hold on   • walk in the woods.

2. Write the correct number.

   a. How many birds did they see?   _____

   b. How many tadpoles did they see?   _____

   c. How many mushrooms did they see?   _____

3. Read the sentence. Choose **Yes** or **No**.

   a. They see a nest in a tree.   ❑ Yes   ❑ No

   b. They trip over a log.   ❑ Yes   ❑ No

   c. They say hello to a speedy spider.   ❑ Yes   ❑ No

   d. They fall in a puddle.   ❑ Yes   ❑ No

Think and Search   Think about what the text says.

1. Which animal in the story croaked?

_____

2. When Granddad and the child hear a *CROAK* and a *QUACK*, they hold hands tightly. Why?

_____

_____

A WALK IN THE WOODS

Use what you know about the text and your own experience.

1. Draw what you would like to happen most if you went for a walk in the woods.

2. Draw what you would not like to happen if you went for a walk in the woods.

A WALK IN THE WOODS

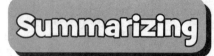

Use the text on page 105 to complete the activity. Draw the missing pictures to finish the story map. Then draw a path to show the walk in the woods. Tell the story to a friend.

Draw Granddad's house.

Draw a nest in a tree.

Draw ten mushrooms.

Draw a wriggling worm.

Draw a speedy spider.

Draw ten tadpoles.

Draw what made a CROAK! and a QUACK!

Common Core State Standards

Standards Correlations

Each lesson meets one or more of the following Common Core State Standards © Copyright 2010. National Governors Association Center for Best Practices and Council of Chief State School Officers. All rights reserved. For more information about the Common Core State Standards, go to http://www.corestandards.org/ or http://www.teachercreated.com/standards.

Reading Literature/Fiction Text Standards	Text Title	Pages
Key Ideas and Details		
ELA.RL.1.1 Ask and answer questions about key details in a text.	A Scary Story	9–13
	On the Riverbank	14–18
	The Sad Goblin	34–38
	The Three Little Pigs	39–43
	Russell the Robot and His Best Buddy	54–58
	Action Rhyme	59–63
	The Wonderful Birthday Gift	64–68
	The Sunflower	69–73
	The Raven and the Swan	74–78
	Why the Bear Has a Stumpy Tail	79–83
	Tilly Tidy-up	84–88
	A Walk in the Woods	104–108
ELA.RL.1.2 Retell stories, including key details, and demonstrate understanding of their central message or lesson.	A Scary Story	9–13
	On the Riverbank	14–18
	The Sad Goblin	34–38
	The Three Little Pigs	39–43
	Russell the Robot and His Best Buddy	54–58
	Action Rhyme	59–63
	The Wonderful Birthday Gift	64–68
	The Sunflower	69–73
	The Raven and the Swan	74–78
	Why the Bear Has a Stumpy Tail	79–83
	Tilly Tidy-up	84–88
	A Walk in the Woods	104–108
ELA.RL.1.3 Describe characters, settings, and major events in a story, using key details.	A Scary Story	9–13
	On the Riverbank	14–18
	The Sad Goblin	34–38
	The Three Little Pigs	39–43
	Russell the Robot and His Best Buddy	54–58
	Action Rhyme	59–63
	The Wonderful Birthday Gift	64–68
	The Sunflower	69–73
	The Raven and the Swan	74–78
	Why the Bear Has a Stumpy Tail	79–83
	Tilly Tidy-up	84–88
	A Walk in the Woods	104–108

Common Core State Standards (cont.)

Reading Literature/Fiction Text Standards (cont.)	Text Title	Pages
Craft and Structure		
ELA.RL.1.4 Identify words and phrases in stories or poems that suggest feelings or appeal to the senses.	The Sad Goblin The Three Little Pigs Action Rhyme	34–38 39–43 59–63
Integration of Knowledge and Ideas		
ELA.RL.1.7 Use illustrations and details in a story to describe its characters, setting, or events.	A Scary Story On the Riverbank The Three Little Pigs Russell the Robot and His Best Buddy Action Rhyme The Wonderful Birthday Gift The Sunflower The Raven and the Swan Why the Bear Has a Stumpy Tail Tilly Tidy-up A Walk in the Woods	9–13 14–18 39–43 54–58 59–63 64–68 69–73 74–78 79–83 84–88 104–108
ELA.RL.1.9 Compare and contrast the adventures and experiences of characters in stories.	The Wonderful Birthday Gift Why the Bear Has a Stumpy Tail	64–68 79–83
Range of Reading and Level of Text Complexity		
ELA.RL.1.10 With prompting and support, read prose and poetry of appropriate complexity for grade 1.	A Scary Story On the Riverbank The Sad Goblin The Three Little Pigs Russell the Robot and His Best Buddy Action Rhyme The Wonderful Birthday Gift The Sunflower The Raven and the Swan Why the Bear Has a Stumpy Tail Tilly Tidy-up A Walk in the Woods	9–13 14–18 34–38 39–43 54–58 59–63 64–68 69–73 74–78 79–83 84–88 104–108

Reading Informational Text/Nonfiction Standards	Text Title	Pages
Key Ideas and Details		
ELA.RI.1.1 Ask and answer questions about key details in a text.	School Assembly Pet Parade Classroom Justin and the Magic Apples Thank You How to Make a Pizza Cartoon The Elephant	19–23 24–28 29–33 44–48 49–53 89–93 94–98 99–103
ELA.RI.1.2 Identify the main topic and retell key details of a text.	School Assembly Pet Parade Classroom Thank You How to Make a Pizza Cartoon The Elephant	19–23 24–28 29–33 49–53 89–93 94–98 99–103
ELA.RI.1.3 Describe the connection between two individuals, events, ideas, or pieces of information in a text.	School Assembly Cartoon The Elephant	19–23 94–98 99–103
Craft and Structure		
ELA.RI.1.4 Ask and answer questions to help determine or clarify the meaning of words and phrases in a text.	Thank You How to Make a Pizza Cartoon The Elephant	49–53 89–93 94–98 99–103
ELA.RI.1.5 Know and use various text features (e.g., headings, tables of contents, glossaries, electronic menus, icons) to locate key facts or information in a text.	School Assembly Pet Parade Justin and the Magic Apples How to Make a Pizza Cartoon	19–23 24–28 44–48 89–93 94–98
ELA.RI.1.6 Distinguish between information provided by pictures or other illustrations and information provided by the words in a text.	School Assembly Pet Parade Classroom Justin and the Magic Apples How to Make a Pizza Cartoon The Elephant	19–23 24–28 29–33 44–48 89–93 94–98 99–103

Reading Informational Text/Nonfiction Standards *(cont.)*	Text Title	Pages
Integration of Knowledge and Ideas		
ELA.RI.1.7 Use the illustrations and details in a text to describe its key ideas.	School Assembly	19–23
	Pet Parade	24–28
	Classroom	29–33
	Justin and the Magic Apples	44–48
	Thank You	49–53
	How to Make a Pizza	89–93
	Cartoon	94–98
	The Elephant	99–103
Range of Reading and Level of Text Complexity		
ELA.RI.1.10 With prompting and support, read informational texts appropriately complex for grade 1.	School Assembly	19–23
	Pet Parade	24–28
	Classroom	29–33
	Justin and the Magic Apples	44–48
	Thank You	49–53
	How to Make a Pizza	89–93
	Cartoon	94–98
	The Elephant	99–103